A Chocolate Bar

Sarah Ridley

GARETH**STEVENS**
PUBLISHING
A Member of the WRC Media Family of Companies

The author and publishers would like to thank the Day Chocolate Company for its help with this book.

Please visit our web site at: **www.garethstevens.com**
For a free color catalog describing Gareth Stevens Publishing's list of high-quality books
and multimedia programs, call 1-800-542-2595 (USA) or 1-800-387-3178 (Canada).
Gareth Stevens Publishing's fax: (414) 332-3567.

Library of Congress Cataloging-in-Publication Data

Ridley, Sarah, 1963- .
    A chocolate bar / by Sarah Ridley.
      p. cm. − (How it's made)
    Includes index.
    ISBN 0-8368-6293-7 (lib. bdg.)
    1. Chocolate processing−Juvenile literature. 2. Chocolate candy−
Juvenile literature.   I. Title.
TP640.R536   2006
664'.153−dc22   2005054075

This North American edition first published in 2006 by
Gareth Stevens Publishing
A Member of the WRC Media Family of Companies
330 West Olive Street, Suite 100
Milwaukee, WI 53212 USA

This U.S. edition copyright © 2006 by Gareth Stevens, Inc.
Original edition copyright © 2005 by Franklin Watts.
First published in Great Britain in 2005 by Franklin Watts,
96 Leonard Street, London EC2A 4XD, United Kingdom.

Series editor: Sarah Peutrill
Art director: Jonathan Hair
Design: Jemima Lumley

Gareth Stevens editor: Dorothy L. Gibbs
Gareth Stevens art direction: Tammy West
Gareth Stevens graphic designer: Charlie Dahl

Photo credits: (t=top, b=bottom, l=left, r=right, c=center)
AKG Images: 17b. Cadburys/News Team International: 21, 23cr, 27tl, 27cr. The Day Chocolate Company: front cover br, back
cover t, 1, 5b, 7tr, 8, 19b, 25t, 26tl, 26cl, 26bl, 27br. Fiona Duale/Divine Chocolate: front cover c, 4t, 11b. Geri Engberd/Image
Works/Topham: 24t. Owen Franken/Corbis: 20t, 27clt. Ron Giling/Still Pictures: 15t. Georgia Glynn-Smith/ABPL: 17t, 19t, 27clb.
Mary Evans Picture Library: 15b, 23b, 24b, 29. Masterfoods: 11t, 22, 27tr. Richard Melloul/Sygma/Corbis: 18, 27bl. Ray Moller/
Franklin Watts: 28 (all). Brian Moody: 6b, 7b, 7tl, 9tl, 10b, 12 (both), 26tr. Museo de America, Madrid/Dagli Orti/Art Archive:
9br. Museum of London/HIP/Topham: 20b. Kim Naylor: 14t, 16 (both), 23tl, 25b, 26cr, 26br. Christine Osborne/Ecoscene: 4bl.
Karen Robinson: back cover b, 6t, 10t, 13t. Karen Robinson/Panos: 31. Sven Torfinn/Panos: 14b. Mireille Vautier/Art Archive:
13b. Peter Wilson/Holt Studios: 5t.

Printed in the United States of America

1 2 3 4 5 6 7 8 9 10 09 08 07 06

Words that appear in the glossary are printed in
boldface type the first time they occur in the text.

Contents

Chocolate is made from cocoa beans.

Cocoa beans grow inside pods on cacao trees. Most cocoa beans come from West Africa, Indonesia, and South America. The chocolate bar in this book was made from cocoa beans that were grown in Ghana, which is a small country in West Africa.

The main ingredients in a milk chocolate bar are cocoa, milk, sugar, and vanilla.

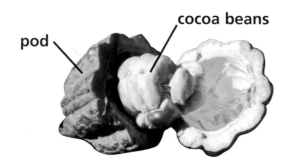

pod

cocoa beans

Most of the cocoa produced in Ghana is sold to the United Kingdom and other European countries, but some is sold to chocolate factories in the United States and Canada. Most of the cocoa from South America is sold to chocolate factories in North America. Cocoa from Indonesia is used mainly in Asia.

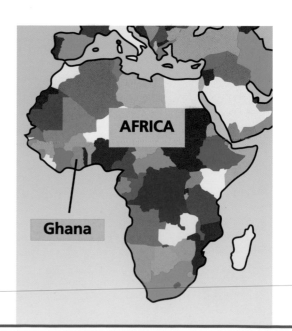

AFRICA

Ghana

Most of the cacao trees in Ghana grow on small family farms. The farmers prepare areas of land in shady places. Then they plant cacao seeds, and cacao trees begin to grow. Cacao trees are often planted in rain forests or under banana or rubber trees.

Three to five years after planting the seeds, the trees burst into blooms, and cocoa pods develop from the flowers.

Each cacao tree produces about ten thousand tiny flowers, but only about twenty to thirty flowers develop into cocoa pods.

The cocoa beans inside the pods are the seeds of the cacao tree.

Where do cacao trees grow?

Cacao trees grow only in places near the Equator, where the weather is always hot and wet. They first grew in the rain forests of South America. Seeds taken from there were planted in equatorial Africa, the Caribbean, Indonesia, Malaysia, and Sri Lanka.

When bean pods are ripe, farmers cut them down.

Every year, each cacao tree produces twenty to thirty pods. Each pod contains about forty cocoa beans. When the pods turn yellow or orange, they are ripe, and the farmers cut them down. Green pods are left on the trees. Ripe cocoa pods are harvested twice a year.

A farmer needs a sharp blade to cut the pods off a cacao tree.

Farmers must be careful not to harm the pods or the tree when they slice off the ripe pods.

Harvested pods are often carried in baskets to a collection point.

cocoa beans in pulp

The farmer splits the pods open with a sharp knife called a machete.

After the pods are harvested, the farmers cut them open. Inside the pods, damp white cocoa beans are resting in pulp.

The pulp and the beans are carefully scraped out of the pods into baskets. At this point, the cocoa beans taste very bitter. The pulp, however, tastes sweet.

When they are first scraped out of the pods, the pulp and the beans are kept together.

The pulp and beans are piled onto leaves.

Farmers use the leaves of plantain trees to help them separate the cocoa beans from the pulp. Plantain trees often grow alongside cacao trees. Plantains are a type of banana.

Farmers pile pulp and beans onto plantain leaves, then they wrap the leaves around each pile to create a kind of package.

The slimy mixture of pulp and beans is piled onto a plantain leaf.

**The leaf packages
are wrapped tightly.**

The leaf packages are left in the sun for five to eight days and become very hot inside. The heat makes the pulp **ferment**, which means that **bacteria** and **yeast** in the pulp multiply. Fermenting releases chemicals that change the flavor of the beans.

The pulp turns to liquid and drains out of the packages. Then the beans are removed.

In the Past

The Maya people, who, from the fourth century, lived in Central America, just south of where Mexico is today, are the first to have left records of a drink made from cocoa beans. They roasted, pounded, and fermented the beans with maize and pepper. The Maya called the beans *cacao*, meaning "food of the gods."

The Aztecs, who settled in Central America in the fourteenth century, learned to make a chocolate drink from the Maya. They poured the drink from up high to make it frothy, or foamy.

The beans are spread out on drying tables.

There is usually no rain in Ghana at harvest time so cocoa beans can be left out in the air to dry. The farmers spread them out on drying tables made of bamboo. The beans must be turned over frequently as they are drying.

On the drying tables, cocoa beans are checked regularly for quality.

Everyone helps with the beans, turning them over so they will dry and picking out any bad beans.

It takes five to twelve days for cocoa beans to dry. As they dry, they shrink in size.

Dried cocoa beans look very different from the damp white beans that farmers scraped out of the pods just two weeks earlier.

Cocoa beans shrink when they dry because they lose most of the water inside them.

What is fair-trade chocolate?

When chocolate and cocoa products are labeled "fair trade," it means that the cocoa beans were grown under good working conditions, the farmers received a fair price for their beans, and they were sure of having a buyer for them. Fair-trade farmers are not as poor as many cocoa farmers have been in the past, or still are today in some parts of the world.

Fair-trade chocolate companies make many types of chocolate bars.

The dried beans are put into sacks.

Farmers and their families not only sort the beans but also fill the sacks and sew them up.

Cocoa beans have to be sorted so that the beans in each sack are all the same quality. So far, the farmers and their families have done everything from planting seeds to sewing up bean sacks. Now, they can sell the beans.

A worker called a recorder weighs each farmer's sacks of beans and checks them for quality. The recorder also arranges to have trucks come to pick up the sacks.

At this point, the recorder pays the farmers half the value of each sack, making sure the price is fair. The recorder will pay the farmers the other half after the beans have been sold.

A recorder checks the weight of each bean sack and keeps careful records.

In the Past

In the fourteenth and fifteenth centuries, the Aztec civilization used cocoa beans the way we use money. Four cocoa beans could buy a pumpkin. Ten cocoa beans could buy a rabbit — to eat! The Aztecs also gave cocoa beans as gifts and used them in religious rituals.

The Aztecs honored visitors such as Spanish adventurer Hernando Cortés (1485–1547) (left) by offering them their highly valued cocoa drink.

The sacks of beans go on a long journey.

It takes two workers to load a sack of cocoa beans onto a truck. Each sack weighs about 135 pounds (62 kilograms)!

Cargo ships can carry hundreds of sacks of cocoa beans.

Trucks carry the sacks of cocoa beans from the farmers' villages to Accra, the capital of Ghana. In Accra, a government cocoa board, known as Cocobod, buys all the sacks of beans.

Because Ghana's farmers belong to a **cooperative**, they will get a better price for their beans than many other farmers will.

Finally, the sacks of beans are loaded onto cargo ships that will take them to ports in Europe or North America.

Workers unload sacks of cocoa beans from ships and pile them up on the docks.

Some cocoa beans go to the Netherlands.

MEILLEUR QUE TOUS LES CHOCOLATS.
T.s.v.p.

In 1828, a Dutchman named Conraad Van Houten invented a machine that could press 50 percent of the cocoa butter out of cocoa beans, leaving dry cocoa cakes and rich cocoa butter. Although some chocolate companies, especially in the United States, have built their own cocoa presses, much of the world's cocoa is still pressed in the Netherlands or in Germany.

An early advertisement for Van Houten cocoa powder called it "The best of all drinking chocolate."

The beans are sorted and roasted.

When cocoa beans reach a chocolate factory, workers split open the sacks and pour the beans into a sorting machine. The machine cleans the beans and sorts them by size.

Factory workers often mix different kinds of cocoa beans to make a tastier chocolate.

Then the beans are roasted to improve the flavor and to destroy any harmful **microorganisms.**

The beans are roasted for 10 to 35 minutes at 250 °Fahrenheit (120 °Celsius) or higher.

After roasting, the cocoa beans are so brittle that the next machines can break them open and blow away the shells with jets of air. This process, which is called winnowing, leaves just cocoa nibs, the inner kernels of the beans.

Leftover bean shells are removed during the winnowing process.

In the Past

Christopher Columbus and Hernando Cortés were both European explorers working for Spain in the early sixteenth century. Columbus brought a few cocoa beans back to Spain in 1502, but it was Cortés who knew the value of cocoa beans. In 1528, he brought back a cargo of beans from Central America with the tools to make the chocolate drink he had been given by the Aztecs. The drink became very popular in Spain and, from there, spread to the rest of Europe.

When Columbus landed at Guanaja, Central America, in 1502, the Aztecs brought him gifts, which included a sack of cocoa beans.

Rollers grind the cocoa nibs into a liquid.

Cocoa nibs are pressed between large rollers to produce a brown liquid called cocoa liquor. This liquid has a very strong chocolate flavor. The cocoa liquor flows from the machine into shallow containers.

At this point, some of the liquid goes to another part of the factory to be blended with other ingredients and made into all kinds of chocolate products. The rest of the liquor goes through a different kind of processing.

Huge steel rollers squash cocoa nibs into a brown liquid.

Cocoa liquor contains a fat called cocoa butter. A powerful machine squeezes this butter out of leftover cocoa liquor, leaving behind solid cakes of cocoa powder, called presscakes.

Cocoa butter is used to help make chocolate. It is also used to make soap and skin creams. Presscakes are ground into cocoa powder.

Trays of finely ground cocoa powder wait to be packaged.

It takes up to a year's crop of cocoa beans from one tree to make one container of cocoa powder.

In the Past

How did chocolate get its name? When the Spanish arrived in Central America, in the 1500s, they met the Aztecs. These Native people offered the Spaniards a drink made from cocoa beans. They called the drink *chocol haa*, which means "hot drink." Living south of the Aztecs, the Maya people used the word *chokola'j*, meaning "to drink chocolate together." When the drink reached Europe, people called it *chocolat* and, finally, *chocolate*.

The liquid cocoa is blended with other ingredients.

Now, the final stage of chocolate production begins. First, cocoa butter is blended into the cocoa liquor. Adding cocoa butter makes the chocolate soft, creamy, and rich tasting. Sugar, vanilla, and powdered or evaporated milk are also added at this stage.

Pouring cocoa butter into cocoa liquor makes chocolate smoother.

This scene shows the inside of a chocolate house in 1787.

In the Past

In the seventeenth century, drinking hot chocolate was a popular pastime in European cities. Some people drank it at home, some at chocolate houses. A chocolate house was a meeting place, or club, where men and women could chat or do business. At the time, poor people could not afford hot chocolate. In the nineteenth century, however, the price of cocoa powder came down. Then, everyone could enjoy hot chocolate.

After all the added ingredients are blended together, the whole mixture is put through another series of steel rollers to make the chocolate smoother.

Next, **conching** begins. The term *conching* comes from the word "conche," which is the name of the machine that is used for this blending process. During conching, the chocolate mixture is stirred constantly at a warm temperature for up to three days. The mixture gradually develops an incredibly smooth texture and an even better flavor.

All the ingredients to make a chocolate bar are mixed together in a huge machine like this one.

The warm chocolate mixture is tempered.

After conching, the chocolate mixture flows into large metal containers known as **tempering** kettles. In these kettles, paddles keep the chocolate moving as it is carefully warmed and cooled several times over several hours.

Tempered chocolate is shiny and very smooth.

Factory workers are very careful during the tempering process. The chocolate could be ruined at this stage. When they are sure that the chocolate is ready, they let it flow into molds.

A factory worker tests the tempered chocolate to find out if it is ready for the molds.

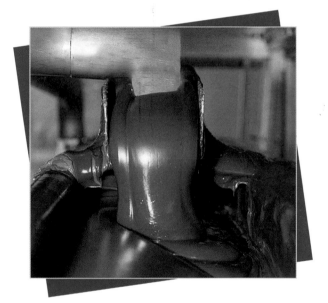

Chocolate flows into a mold.

In the Past

In 1847, in England, J. S. Fry added cocoa butter to a mixture of cocoa powder and sugar to make the first true chocolate bar. At first, only the wealthy could afford this expensive treat.

A 1907 advertisement for Fry's chocolate

The chocolate bars stay in their molds until they have cooled. Then the bars are tipped out onto a **conveyor belt**.

The chocolate bar is checked for quality.

A factory worker checks every bar of chocolate to make sure all the bars are good enough to sell.

As the conveyor belt passes in front her, this factory worker looks for poor-quality chocolate bars.

CHOC-FULL OF GOODNESS !

Is chocolate good for you?

Chocolate can be good for you as long as you do not eat too much of it! It is high in fat and sugar so it could make you gain weight. Scientists have discovered, however, that chocolate, especially dark chocolate, contains chemicals that can protect your heart against disease and help prevent cancer.

In the past, chocolate companies were allowed to advertise chocolate as a healthy food.

It takes a whole crop of cocoa beans from just one tree to make four to six bars of delicious Divine chocolate!

Finally, machines seal each bar in foil and cover the foil with a paper wrapper. The chocolate bars are packed in boxes and loaded onto trucks that will take them to warehouses and stores so they can be sold to chocolate-lovers everywhere.

Stores and shops of all kinds offer a wide range of chocolate bars. Both Divine and Dubble chocolate bars are fair-trade chocolate products.

How a Chocolate Bar Is Made

1. Cocoa pods grow on cacao trees.

4. The farmers spread the beans out on drying tables.

2. The farmers harvest ripe pods and split them open.

5. The beans are shipped to a cocoa processing factory.

3. The pulp and beans are wrapped in plantain leaves and left to ferment.

6. Various machines clean, roast, and winnow the beans, leaving cocoa nibs.

10. Sugar and milk are added to the chocolate mixture.

11. The chocolate is conched, then tempered, being stirred all the time as it is warmed and cooled.

9. Cocoa butter is added to the cocoa liquor to make a smooth mixture.

12. Warm, tempered chocolate flows into molds, where it stays until it is cool.

8. Powerful machines squeeze the cocoa butter out of some of the cocoa liquor, leaving cocoa powder.

7. Rollers squash the cocoa nibs to make cocoa liquor.

Divine
MILK CHOCOLATE
HEAVENLY MILK CHOCOLATE
WITH A HEART
NET WT. 3½ OZ (100g)

13. The bars are tipped out of the molds, then wrapped and packed — ready to eat!

More Ways to Use Cocoa

**How many of these ways
have you eaten chocolate?**

chocolate shapes

chocolate
muffins

chocolate ice cream

chocolate rolls

chocolate cookies

Chocolate products use only the cocoa nibs at the center of the cocoa bean. Many other products use the rest of the cocoa pod. Here are a few examples of those products:

- The husks of cocoa pods are used to make animal feed. They are also used to make soaps and fertilizer.
- Juice from the pulp of cocoa pods is collected during fermentation and is bottled to be sold as a drink.
- The shells of cocoa pods are used by gardeners to improve the soil.
- Cocoa butter is used to make soaps and moisturizing skin creams.

Famous Chocolate Companies

Some of today's best-known chocolate companies in England and North America were started at a time when many people suffered with poor housing and working conditions. The people who started these companies believed in taking care of their workers and treating them fairly.

In 1879, George Cadbury built a new factory for his chocolate company. Called Bournville, it was near Birmingham, in the United Kingdom. Cadbury also built a village at Bournville, with houses, shops, and schools for his workers.

Bournville offered Cadbury workers both jobs and housing.

Other British chocolate companies, including Rowntree and Terry's, of York, also built houses, schools, and training colleges.

In the United States, Milton Hershey built the famous factory town of Hershey, Pennsylvania, with an amusement park and a zoo for his workers' enjoyment!

Fair Trade and Kuapa Kokoo

You may have noticed fair-trade labels on some of the food products you buy. In addition to chocolate, you can purchase fair-trade bananas, rice, honey, coffee, and many other products. Most of these goods are grown in poor areas of the world.

Kuapa Kokoo is the name for a group of cocoa farmers in Ghana, West Africa, who joined together to form a cooperative. *Kuapa Kokoo* means "good cocoa farmers" in Twi, which is the local language. The Kuapa Kokoo's motto is *PaPa Paa*, which means "the best of the best."

Fair-Trade Labels

A fair-trade label means that

- farmers receive fair, fixed prices for their goods
- cocoa buyers pay a "social premium," which provides money to farmers' villages and communities for improving services such as health care and water
- farmers have long-term contracts with the buyers of their goods
- farmers work in good conditions and have a say in how the cooperative is run

Different countries have different fair-trade labels.

 United States and Canada

 United Kingdom

The Kuapa Kokoo cooperative works for the good of all of its 45,000 members to help them grow and sell their cocoa beans. All the cocoa sold by the cooperative's members is grown under fair-trade conditions.

The Day Chocolate Company

Kuapa Kokoo owns one-third of The Day Chocolate Company, which makes Divine and Dubble chocolate bars. Any extra money that the company makes is shared by the farmers in Ghana who grew the cocoa.

The benefits of Kuapa Kokoo help Ghana's cocoa farmers and their families enjoy safer and healthier living conditions than many other cocoa farmers.

The Benefits of Belonging to Kuapa Kokoo

- The farmers earn more as a cooperative because they have better selling power and are more efficient at doing business.
- At the end of the year, any profit made by the cooperative is divided up and paid as a bonus to each farmer.
- Kuapa Kokoo pays for improvements, such as better water supplies, in the farmers' villages and communities.
- Because Kuapa Kokoo buys many tools at one time, it can get them at a lower price, which can be passed on to its members.
- Kuapa Kokoo organizes training and education for its members.

Glossary

bacteria – the name for many different types of very small, single-celled living things that live everywhere

conching – the part of the chocolate-making process during which cocoa liquor, blended with other ingredients, is stirred constantly at a warm temperature to improve its texture and flavor

conveyor belt – a constantly moving belt of rubber that is used in factories to move items from one production area to another

cooperative – a group of people who join together to improve working conditions, wages, and the overall quality of life for all members of the group

ferment – to go through a chemical breakdown, often using yeast, that is accompanied by bubbling due to the release of a gas such as carbon dioxide

microorganisms – microscopically tiny living things, some of which cause diseases

tempering – part of the chocolate-making process during which a mixture of chocolate and other ingredients is alternately heated and cooled to develop a shiny appearance and better flavor

yeast – a group of tiny fungi that use sugar to grow. When yeast grows in cocoa leaf parcels, the pulp and beans ferment to develop the cocoa's flavor.

Index